The Masses of Advent

The Masses of Advent

A Helpful Guide to the Scripture Readings
For the Sundays and Weekdays

Cassian A. Miles, O.F.M.

Weekday commentaries reprinted from *Alert to God's Word: Ready-to-Read Scripture Guides for Weekday Masses* by Rev. Cassian A. Miles, O.F.M., with the permission of The Liturgical Press, Order of St. Benedict, Inc.

Cover and book design by Julie Van Leeuwen.

Cover photograph by Cliff Koehler.

SBN 0-912228-59-8

© 1979, The Order of Friars Minor of the Province of the Most Holy Name (USA).

Printed by St. Anthony Messenger Press.

Table of Contents

First Week of Advent 1
Second Week of Advent 6
Third Week of Advent 11
Fourth Week of Advent 16

Advent Sunday Cycles

A		1980	1983	1986	1989
B		1981	1984	1987	1990
C	1979	1982	1985	1988	1991

How to Use This Pamphlet

Welcome to the fascinating world of the Scripture readings for the Advent season!

Yes, "fascinating" — because you will find that in these Scripture readings the liturgy achieves, each day, a beautiful unity and interrelatedness of the texts for the Old Testament lesson, the responsorial psalm, the New Testament lesson and the Gospel.

Unless you are aware of this fact, however, the readings for each day might seem to be only a casual collection of assorted passages from the Bible, without any particular theme to link them to one another.

This pamphlet has been written to help you find out for yourself what appears to be the dominant theme unifying the readings for each day of Advent. In other words, the theme suggested is only one approach. Once you develop a feel for how the Scriptures fit together, you may well find other themes of your own. That's fine. No one can pretend to have identified *the* one and only theme for each day. The Scriptures are so diversified and the interrelated meanings are so rich that you will almost certainly discover themes of your own as you progress through the Advent season.

But at least this pamphlet will have pointed you in the direction of recognizing *themes*. That's why I believe this will be a fascinating experience for you as you explore, day by day, the many meanings that God's Word offers for you and the life you live as a Christian.

This pamphlet is definitely not a scholarly Scripture commentary on individual readings. There is plenty of help available in that area elsewhere. Nor does it attempt to give pious meditations or reflections for this Advent season with the Scriptures as our starting point.

The purpose throughout is simply to explain one way the texts relate to one another and to identify the unifying theme which connects them. I feel, in all humility, that this will help the Scriptures themselves to speak to you — not necessarily in a passage's literal meaning, but in the sense in which it supports and develops the day's dominant theme.

So the vantage point will be that of the liturgy itself as we explore together the texts chosen for each particular day. Since the Church has provided no official explanation of this selection process, I have felt free to suggest what seems a reasonable interpretation of the links which bind each day's texts together.

In view of this reasoning, how will you put this pamphlet to work and by doing so get the most spiritual benefit from it? Various approaches are possible depending on your circumstances and the time you have available.

If you can, the ideal approach is to read these guides to the daily Scripture readings for Advent during leisure moments at home before going to Mass. Even read them a second time to get a feel for the direction the theme seems to be taking. Then turn to your Bible. Although references to the texts for each day are cited in their proper sequence, I suggest that you turn to the passages *in the order in which they are dealt with* in the Scripture guide itself.

For example, if the guide begins by commenting on the Gospel, turn first to that Gospel text in your Bible and read through it slowly and prayerfully. If the guide deals next with the Old Testament lesson, turn to that and read it, continuing to keep the suggested theme in mind. At times you will find that the liturgy brings together passages from different sections of a chapter in order to structure a reading for the Mass. In such a case, you can choose to read either the full passage from the Bible — even the entire chapter — or the shortened liturgical form. This kind of selection occurs most often in the responsorial psalms, where the liturgy often unifies scattered verses into one responsorial composite.

On the other hand, if you are fortunate enough to own or have access to a lectionary or a missal that gives the full texts of the day's readings, you will find reflecting on the texts that much easier. Weekday missalettes do not usually carry the texts of the Scripture readings, but those for Sunday often do. So if on a Sunday you can get to Mass a bit early, take this pamphlet with you, and you will be able to examine the texts right in the missalette.

If you cannot find time to read the Scriptures before going to Mass, you can still use this pamphlet to help you listen more fruitfully to God's Word, because you will be able to listen with greater understanding. Having read beforehand the Scripture guide for the day, perhaps even twice to let the theme impress itself on you, you will find you can make a lot more sense out of the Scripture passages as the celebrant or lector proclaims God's Word to your congregation.

Possibly sometime later on in the day you may have an opportunity to pick up your Bible and review the readings at your own pace for still further enrichment from the treasure of God's Word.

The Sunday readings recur in a three-year cycle rather than annually like the weekday readings. Refer to the Scripture guides for Cycle A in the years 1980, 1983, 1986 and every three years after that. Use Cycle B for 1981, 1984, 1987 and so on. Use Cycle C for 1979, 1982, 1985 and each third year following.

If you find this pamphlet helpful, you may wish to use a similar one which has been prepared for the Lenten season: *The Masses of Lent: A Helpful Guide to the Scripture Readings and Themes for Each Day* from St. Anthony Messenger Press. The Scripture guides for Advent and Lent (weekdays only) are taken from a handy pocket-size book titled *Alert to God's Word*, Scripture guides for *all* weekday Masses of the year, published by The Liturgical Press, Collegeville, Minnesota 56321, at $5.85.

It is my sincere prayer that your use of these Scripture guides will make this liturgical season rich in meaning for you, and profitable for your growth in Christ. At the same time, I think you will be greatly enriched by discovering the treasures that lie hidden for all of us in God's Word. For my part, I have enjoyed unearthing some of them for you.

Finally, I would be seriously remiss in not acknowledging the incisive editorial comments of my close friend and consultant, Mr. James C. G. Conniff, without whom the purpose of this pamphlet would have fallen far short of its pastoral goal.

Fr. Cassian A. Miles, O.F.M.

New York City

First Week of Advent

FIRST SUNDAY OF ADVENT — Cycle A

READING I   Is. 2:1-5   RESP. Ps. 122:1-2, 3-4, 4-5, 6-7, 8-9
READING II Rom. 13:11-14
GOSPEL   Matthew 24:37-44

    Today's Advent readings bring to a climax the same themes that adorn the Scriptures for the concluding Sundays of each Church year: the end of the world and our Christian hope for the final coming of Christ. Thus we discover that one liturgical season dovetails into the other. The first passage gives us a *pre-Christian* view of those "days to come," when our human history will have reached its final stage. The prophet Isaiah sees all the nations of the world coming on a pilgrimage to "the mountain of the Lord's house" — a symbol of the Temple in Jerusalem, where God dwelt among his people. There God will teach them his ways. Once they "walk in his paths," peace will finally come. The responsorial psalm takes up the themes of the pilgrimage to God's house and eventual peace among all peoples. Paul directs our attention to the day of "our salvation," another reference to the end of time, and gives practical advice on how to prepare for it. The Gospel itself warns us to keep alert, because that final coming of Christ will occur suddenly, bringing about a separation of the saved and the lost.

FIRST SUNDAY OF ADVENT — Cycle B

READING I   Is. 63:16-17, 19; 64:2-7   RESP. Ps. 80:2-3, 15-16, 18-19
READING II 1 Cor. 1:3-9
GOSPEL   Mark 13:33-37

    Today's Advent readings bring to a climax the same themes that enrich the Scriptures for the concluding Sundays of each Church year: the end of the world and our Christian hope for the final coming of Christ. In this way, we find that one liturgical season flows into the next. The Old Testament lesson speaks of God's return, his coming down from the heavens, and how we should prepare our hearts for him. The prophet prays that God "might meet us doing right," but painfully admits that such is not the case. The chosen people have turned their backs on God, as perhaps we have done ourselves in some way. Sensitive to this, the liturgy uses a responsorial psalm asking for God's help. We pray that the Lord may "make us turn to" him, so that "we shall be saved." We then promise that "we will no more withdraw from" the Lord. In the second reading, Paul also challenges us to live out our waiting for "the revelation of Jesus" in such a way that God will find us "blameless on the day" when he comes. The Gospel itself urges us to stay awake spiritually, as we wait for the Lord's return.

FIRST SUNDAY OF ADVENT — Cycle C

READING I Jer. 33:14-16
READING II 1 Thes. 3:12—4:2
GOSPEL Luke 21:25-28, 34-36
RESP. Ps. 25:4-5, 8-9, 10, 14

Today's Advent readings bring to a climax a theme that fills the Scriptures for the concluding Sundays of each Church year: our Christian hope for the final coming of Christ. Thus one liturgical season dovetails into the next. The particular note of expectant *waiting* for the Messiah runs through all of today's texts. As we read the Old Testament lesson, we recall that the Jewish people had to wait many centuries for God to "fulfill the promise" to save them through his Messiah. Jeremiah describes him as a "just shoot" or new growth on the family tree of King David. The prophet's claim that the Messiah "shall do what is right and just" finds an echo in the responsorial psalm verse, "He guides the humble to justice." The psalm then directs us to the future. We pray that God our savior may guide us, as we "wait all the day" for Christ's return. Paul exhorts us to live "blameless and holy lives," as we await "the coming of our Lord Jesus." The Gospel summons us to "be on guard" with hearts prepared by prayer and moderate Christian living for the appearance of "the Son of Man" in "great power and glory."

MONDAY OF THE FIRST WEEK OF ADVENT — Cycle A

READING I Is. 4:2-6
GOSPEL Matthew 8:5-11
RESP. Ps. 122:1-2, 3-4, (4-5, 6-7), 8-9

Today's readings tell us about the age of the Messiah that the coming of Jesus into the world made a reality and which we recall in this Advent season. In the first passage, the prophet Isaiah looks forward to that age during which "the survivors of Israel" would live. These are the Jewish people who have survived a difficult time when God purified them because they had turned away from him. The prophet describes the blessings that the Jews enjoy in this age of the Messiah — rich harvests in the land, the favor of being God's holy people, and the protecting shelter of God's love over their lives. The responsorial psalm highlights these blessings in the verse, "May peace be within your walls, prosperity in your buildings." In the Gospel, Jesus also refers to the time when people from east and west will find a place at the banquet in God's kingdom.

MONDAY OF THE FIRST WEEK OF ADVENT — Cycles B & C

READING I Is. 2:1-5 **RESP. Ps.** 122:1-2, 3-4, (4-5, 6-7), 8-9
GOSPEL Matthew 8:5-11

At the weekday Masses of Advent, the liturgy selects Scripture readings that emphasize important themes of this season. Today's readings remind us that Jesus came as the promised Messiah to open the gates of God's kingdom to all men. The first passage looks forward to that day by describing how "all nations shall stream" toward "the mountain of the Lord's house." This mountain is the place where the Jews built the temple in Jerusalem. In this way, the liturgy teaches us that the Church is the new city of Jerusalem that welcomes all men into its fold. The responsorial psalm also portrays the people of all lands saying, "Let us go to the house of the Lord" in Jerusalem, which once again stands for God's kingdom. Then in the Gospel Jesus points out how not only the Jews but all men "will come from the east and the west" and find a place at the banquet in God's kingdom.

TUESDAY OF THE FIRST WEEK OF ADVENT

READING 1 Is. 11:1-10 **RESP. Ps.** 72:1, 7-8, 12-13, 17
GOSPEL Luke 10:21-24

The first Scripture reading for today's Mass directs our attention to the theme of the Messiah as King of Israel. The prophet Isaiah explains that once God has chastised the kingdom of Judah for its sins, the Lord will raise up a new king from the line of David. God will bestow on him all the qualities of the ideal king. His rule will begin the age of peace and justice when all nations will accept God. A reference near the end of this passage to the animals living in peace with one another suggests that the age of the Messiah will be a paradise restored. The responsorial psalm highlights this future messianic age in the refrain, "Justice shall flourish in his time, and fullness of peace forever." In the Gospel, Jesus tells his disciples that their knowledge of God's kingdom is what the prophets and kings of ages past looked forward to and spoke about.

WEDNESDAY OF THE FIRST WEEK OF ADVENT

Reading I   Is. 25:6-10   RESP. Ps. 23:1-3, 3-4, 5, 6
GOSPEL   Matthew 15:29-37

Today's Scripture readings present the theme of a feast that God will provide for all who have kept faith with him when his kingdom achieves its final victory at the end of time. This important message should offer hope to our hearts in this Advent season when we look forward to the final coming of Christ. The first reading tells us about a feast that God will give on his sacred mountain in Jerusalem for "all peoples" when sorrow and death will be no more. The responsorial psalm appropriately refers to God "spreading a table" for all who serve him faithfully. The Gospel describes how Jesus fed a crowd with only seven loaves and a few fish. This miracle suggests the bread of his own body that Jesus gave us at the Last Supper. Our Lord told his disciples then that he would share a banquet with them one day in the kingdom of his Father — a banquet we anticipate at this Mass.

THURSDAY OF THE FIRST WEEK OF ADVENT

READING I   Is. 26:1-6   RESP. Ps. 118:1, 8-9, 19-21, 25-27
GOSPEL   Matthew 7:21, 24-27

The Scripture readings for today's Mass ask us to consider to what extent we really place our trust in God and make him the firm foundation of our lives. In the first passage, the prophet Isaiah reveals that God is someone whom we can rely on with complete confidence. Isaiah's opening words depict God as setting up the walls of the city he loves and afterwards protecting it. But the prophet reminds us that God does this because the people who live in the city are faithful to him. On the other hand, God is like a rock who crushes those people who are proud and who trust in material riches rather than in him. The responsorial psalm accents the theme of the Mass by pointing out the rewards that come to the man who trusts in the Lord. The Gospel completes this theme by showing us a man who builds his life on the firm foundation of God's sacred words.

FRIDAY OF THE FIRST WEEK OF ADVENT

READING I   Is. 29:17-24   **RESP. Ps.** 27:1, 4, 13-14
GOSPEL   Matthew 9:27-31

Restoring sight to the blind is the theme that unifies the Scripture readings for today's Mass. However, this theme doesn't emphasize just the physical fact of being able to see again. The liturgy uses this wondrous change from blindness to sight to teach us, instead, about our faith and the way it ties us personally to Jesus. The Bible often treats blindness as a symbol for a person's lack of faith. In the first Scripture reading, the prophet Isaiah promises the cure of those who are physically and spiritually blind in the future age of the Messiah. Through the public ministry of Jesus, that longed-for age became a reality and is still with us. The responsorial psalm emphasizes this theme by proclaiming, "The Lord is my light," and by stating our desire to "gaze on the loveliness of the Lord." The Gospel story of the two blind men reminds us that faith delivers us from spiritual blindness.

SATURDAY OF THE FIRST WEEK OF ADVENT

READING I   Is. 30:19-21, 23-26   **RESP. Ps.** 147:1-2, 3-4, 5-6
GOSPEL   Matthew 9:35—10:1, 6-8

The Scripture readings for today's Mass focus on the theme of God taking care of his people. In the first passage, we hear God promising that he will not abandon them. He indicates through vivid word-pictures how he will give them prosperity. He will relieve their sufferings, their hunger, their want. He will grant abundant crops and cattle. Through such heart-warming images of the messianic times, the prophet Isaiah tries to bring hope and encouragement to the people to sustain them in times of trial. The responsorial psalm echoes this theme by referring to various ways that God will care for his people through his power and wisdom. The Gospel completes this theme by showing how the heart of Jesus was moved with pity at the sight of all the sick who came to have him heal them.

Second Week of Advent

SECOND SUNDAY OF ADVENT — Cycle A

READING I Is. 11:1-10   RESP. Ps. 72:1-2, 7-8, 12-13, 17
READING II Rom. 15:4-9
GOSPEL   Matthew 3:1-12

    Each of today's Scriptures contains time references to the first coming of Christ. The Old Testament lesson refers to "that day" when the Messiah will appear as a descendant from the family tree or "stump of Jesse," the father of King David. The Messiah will minister to the poor and afflicted, and his rule will bring such wonderful days that even "the baby shall play by the cobra's den" without harm. The responsorial psalm also points to the "time" of "the king's son," an image of the Messiah, and accents how he shall rescue "the poor" and "the afflicted." After directing us to the time before Christ's appearance, Paul affirms that Jesus "became the servant of the Jews," a likeness to Isaiah's picture of the Messiah. We also find a link between the prophet's vision that "the Gentiles shall seek out" the Messiah's dwelling and Paul's reference to "the Gentiles glorifying God because of his mercy." In the Gospel, the fiery preaching of John the Baptizer signals that finally "the reign of God is at hand." The One who will "burn the chaff," symbol of the wicked, confirms Isaiah's image of the Messiah "slaying the wicked."

SECOND SUNDAY OF ADVENT — Cycle B

READING I Is. 40:1-5, 9-11   RESP. Ps. 85:9-10, 11-12, 13-14
READING II 2 Pt. 3:8-14
GOSPEL   Mark 1:1-8

    Three of today's Scripture readings center on the coming of Christ as the long-awaited Messiah. In the Gospel, we find John the Baptizer preaching in the desert as the herald of the Lord. John's baptism that leads to "the forgiveness of sins" ties in to the promise in the first reading that God will one day comfort his people and expiate their guilt. The Gospel writer Mark sees John as the fulfillment of the prophet's vision of the herald crying out in the desert and preparing the Messiah's way, since he begins his text by quoting from Isaiah. John, like Isaiah's herald, fears "not to cry out to the cities of Judah: 'Here is your God!' " John's preaching theme of "one more powerful than I" links to the Old Testament promise, "Here comes with power the Lord God." The theme of the herald is echoed in the responsorial psalm in the verse "Justice shall walk before him," as well as John's proclamation of salvation to "those who fear" God. The second reading sounds another Advent keynote, that we are looking forward to Christ's final coming. Peter exhorts us to prepare for this sudden "day of the Lord" by living a dedicated Christian life.

SECOND SUNDAY OF ADVENT — Cycle C

READING I Bar. 5:1-9
READING II Phil. 1:4-6, 8-11
GOSPEL Luke 3:1-6
RESP. Ps. 126:1-2, 2-3, 4-5, 6

Three of today's Scriptures deal with the coming of Christ as the long-awaited Messiah. In the Gospel we find John the Baptizer preaching in the desert as the herald of the Lord. John's baptism that leads to "the forgiveness of sins" ties in to the prophet Baruch's portrayal of the Jewish people (symbolized by Jerusalem) preparing to return from exile because God has forgiven them. John's preaching allows "all mankind to see the salvation of God," fulfilling Baruch's vision that God would "show all the earth" the new splendor of his forgiven people. The Gospel writer Luke quotes from Isaiah about the herald who levels every mountain or obstacle in the Messiah's way. The first passage offers a matching verse, "that every lofty mountain be made low." The responsorial psalm's joyful tone echoes the promise of "God leading Israel in joy" and the rejoicing of the released captives. Baruch's image of Jerusalem standing upon the heights, looking to the east, suggests the dawn of Christ's final coming and leads into Paul's theme. He urges us to prepare for that day "with a clear conscience and blameless conduct."

MONDAY OF THE SECOND WEEK OF ADVENT

READING I Is. 35:1-10
GOSPEL Luke 5:17-26
RESP. Ps. 85:9-10, 11-12, 13-14

Today's readings apply to the Advent theme of Jesus as the long-awaited Messiah. We discover in the first passage the kind of blessings that God will give to his people in the age of the Messiah. Among these, God will "make firm the knees that are weak," and then "the lame will leap like a stag." In the Gospel, we find Jesus performing a miracle for a crippled man that makes those blessings a reality for the people of his time. After forgiving the man's sins, our Lord heals the paralytic's weak limbs so that he can take up his mat and walk home, giving thanks to God. The first reading also promises that in the age of the Messiah the people "will see the glory of the Lord." We note in the Gospel that after our Lord's miracle, the crowd praises God for the wonder they have seen. The responsorial psalm echoes another theme of the reading, that "our God will come to save us."

TUESDAY OF THE SECOND WEEK OF ADVENT

READING I   Is. 40:1-11   RESP. Ps. 96:1-2, 3, 10, 11-12, 13
GOSPEL   Matthew 18:12-14

The first Scripture reading tells how God called the prophet Isaiah to bring comfort to God's people. This passage mentions a voice that cries out, "In the desert prepare the way of the Lord." This same expression occurs frequently in the prayers throughout the Advent season. It describes the mission of John the Baptist to prepare the way for the Messiah. Near the end of this reading, the prophet tells of a shepherd-king who "feeds his flock." It is a theme that calls to mind the image of Jesus as a shepherd which we find in today's Gospel. Our Lord uses the image of one sheep that has gone astray to teach us God's compassion for sinners. The responsorial psalm that we pray between these readings proclaims God's coming to us in all his strength and majesty — another important Advent theme.

WEDNESDAY OF THE SECOND WEEK OF ADVENT

READING I   Is. 40:25-31   RESP. Ps. 103:1-2, 3-4, 8, 10
GOSPEL   Matthew 11:28-30

The Scripture readings for today's Mass teach us that God gives us the strength we need to face difficult situations, discouragement, and loneliness. The first passage describes a period of discouragement for the Jewish people — the sixth century before Christ when the Babylonians had taken them into exile. The Jews fell into despair, thinking that God had abandoned them. That was why God sent a prophet to remind his beloved people that the Lord is the creator of all things and will not abandon those he loves. The responsorial psalm describes various ways that God bestows benefits upon his people. In thanksgiving, we pray, "O bless the Lord, my soul." The Gospel also deals with the theme of God comforting his people in time of trial. Jesus invites us to come to him with all our problems and he will refresh us.

THURSDAY OF THE SECOND WEEK OF ADVENT

READING I   Is. 41:13-20   **RESP. Ps. 145:1, 9, 10-11, 12-13**
GOSPEL   Matthew 11:11-15

Today's Scripture readings present two themes of the Advent season — first, the blessings of the future age of the Messiah which the Jews looked forward to, and second, John the Baptist's preaching to prepare men for the Messiah's coming. In the first passage, God speaks as the Holy One of Israel to his chosen people in their Babylonian exile. God tells them not to fear because he will restore their land to them. In images familiar to the agricultural society of that time, the Lord describes the many ways he will enrich Israel. Today's liturgy suggests that we apply these images to the spiritual blessings we have experienced in our life of faith and be grateful for them. The responsorial psalm is a prayer thanking God for his kindness to us. In the Gospel, Jesus praises John the Baptist but teaches that the least member of God's kingdom is greater than this saint.

FRIDAY OF THE SECOND WEEK OF ADVENT

READING I   Is. 48:17-19   **RESP. Ps. 1:1-2, 3, 4, 6**
GOSPEL   Matthew 11:16-19

Today's Scripture readings present two quite different ways in which men relate to God. The first passage shows us the way of the faithful and the blessings that come to them. God promises to give prosperity to the Jewish people if they remain true to him. The Gospel indicates the way of the faithless and their punishment. Our Lord tells a parable in which the Jews are like domineering children at play in the marketplace of life. They are angry because John the Baptist and Jesus — their playmates — will not play their game of easy living and looking down on sinners. As a result, the Jews fail to realize that this is the very last chance that God will give them to reform their lives. The responsorial psalm between these readings is another contrasting picture of two men — one who is faithful to God's ways and one who is not.

SATURDAY OF THE SECOND WEEK OF ADVENT

READING I   Sirach 48:1-4, 9-11   **RESP.** Ps. 80:2-3, 15-16, 18-19
GOSPEL   Matthew 17:10-13

In today's readings we discover the relationship between the prophet Elijah and John the Baptist, the last in the line of the prophets, who prepared the way for Christ. The first passage declares that Elijah would return to soften the hearts of the people to welcome the Messiah. That was why the Jews at the time of Christ looked forward to Elijah's return as a sign that the Messiah would shortly deliver them from their Roman oppressors. As the Gospel begins, the disciples of Jesus have just witnessed his transfiguration on Mount Tabor. Moses and Elijah had appeared, talking with Jesus. The disciples then ask when Elijah will return. Jesus indicates that Elijah had already come to them through John the Baptist. The responsorial psalm proclaims the familiar cry of the Advent season, "Rouse your power, and come to save us."

Third Week of Advent

THIRD SUNDAY OF ADVENT — Cycle A

READING I   Is. 35:1-6, 10   RESP. Ps. 146:6-7, 8-9, 9-10
READING II Jas. 5:7-10
GOSPEL   Matthew 11:2-11

In today's Gospel summary of the healing ministry of Jesus, our Christian faith discovers how our Lord fulfilled the Old Testament promises that the Messiah would bring an age of blessings to the Jewish people. We listen with the disciples of John the Baptizer as Jesus tells how the miracles he performs invite belief that God is present and at work in his ministry. "The blind recover their sight, cripples walk, the deaf hear, dead men are raised to life." Our Lord's answer echoes the language of the first reading. The prophet promises that when God comes to save his people, "then will the eyes of the blind be opened, the ears of the deaf be cleared," and other healings of flesh and spirit will occur. The responsorial psalm presents parallel examples of these saving acts of the Lord, who "raises up those that were bowed down." Yet while concentrating on the first coming of Christ, the liturgy does not allow us to lose sight of his final coming. Therefore, we find James in the second lesson urging us to await that time by living at peace with others and practicing the patience of a farmer and the ancient prophets.

THIRD SUNDAY OF ADVENT — Cycle B

READING I   Is. 61:1-2, 10-11   RESP. Ps. Luke 1:46-48, 49-50, 53-54
READING II 1 Thes. 5:16-24
GOSPEL   John 1:6-8, 19-28

The joy that fills our hearts as we look forward to the liturgical celebration of the birth of Jesus finds echoes in the Scriptures for today's Mass. In the Old Testament lesson, God's prophet looks forward to proclaiming to the captive Jewish people in Babylon the "glad tidings" that the Lord will soon secure their return to the homeland in Israel.

The people rejoice "heartily in the Lord" at this news in words that parallel the way Mary rejoiced, when she visited Elizabeth, in the favors God had bestowed on her. For this reason, the liturgy selects an abbreviated form of Mary's hymn of joy, the Magnificat, for our response to the reading. Paul, too, underlines this theme of rejoicing in the advice he gives to the Christian community at Thessalonica. Also appropriate to this Advent season is his prayer that the lives of the Thessalonians may be "irreproachable at the coming of our Lord Jesus Christ." In the Gospel, John the Baptizer's answer to the priests and Levites from Jerusalem sounds a note of joyful looking forward to the coming of the Messiah, whom John judged himself unworthy to serve.

THIRD SUNDAY OF ADVENT — Cycle C

READING I Zeph. 3:14-18 **RESP.** Ps. Is. 12:2-3, 4, 5-6
READING II Phil. 4:4-7
GOSPEL Luke 3:10-18

The joy that fills our hearts as we look forward to the Church's celebration of the birth of Jesus finds echoes in today's Scripture readings. How appropriate to the coming Christmas season are the prophet Zephaniah's words, "The Lord is in your midst, you have no further misfortune to fear." We discover the meaning of the Nativity in Zephaniah's promise that God will "renew you in his love." Our response to this reading borrows a song from the prophet Isaiah, who invites us to "cry out with joy and gladness" over this same intimate presence of God among his beloved people. In the second lesson, the liturgy once again urges us, through the words of Paul, to fill our hearts with rejoicing at the promise that "the Lord himself is near." We will shortly kneel before the Savior's crib and present our needs "in every form of prayer." The Gospel shows us John the Baptizer telling the crowds who flock to him at the Jordan River how to find true joy — not in satisfying themselves, but by caring for the needs of others. Like those people we are "full of anticipation" for the Lord who baptizes us "in the Holy Spirit."

MONDAY OF THE THIRD WEEK OF ADVENT

If today is December 17 or later, omit these readings and turn to pages 17-21.

READING I   Num. 24:2-7, 15-17   RESP. Ps. 25:4-5, 6-7, 8-9
GOSPEL   Matthew 21:23-27

Today's first Scripture reading presents a figure from the days of the Old Testament, a man named **Balaam**. The Spirit of the Lord inspires Balaam to utter oracles or prophecies about the future of the Jewish people and the age of the Messiah. We hear **Balaam** declare that "a star shall advance from Jacob, and a staff shall rise from Israel." The terms "star" and "staff" are symbols for the royal power of a king. From very early times, both Jewish and Christian commentators on this passage have applied this prophecy to the Messiah. We may regard the responsorial psalm refrain as **Balaam's** prayer that God might prepare his heart to speak to the people. He pleads, "Teach me your ways, O Lord." In the Gospel, the chief priests question Jesus about his right to teach the way he does. Like Balaam, our Lord speaks on the authority of another, his Father, and not on his own.

TUESDAY OF THE THIRD WEEK OF ADVENT

If today is December 17 or later, omit these readings and turn to pages 17-21.

READING I   Zeph. 3:1-2, 9-13   RESP. Ps. 34:2-3, 6-7, 17-18, 19, 23
GOSPEL   Matthew 21:28-32

Both Scripture readings for today's Mass reveal how God rebukes the Jewish people of the Old and New Testaments for not cooperating with his grace. The first passage begins with the prophet Zephaniah's reproach to the city of Jerusalem — a symbol for the whole nation. At that time, tyranny ruled the city and a religious outlook had practically disappeared in the wake of gross injustices. Zephaniah then promises that God will spare a small number of people who were faithful to him. The responsorial psalm refers to two themes of the reading in the verses "the Lord hears the cry of the poor" and "the Lord destroys the remembrance of evildoers." In the Gospel, Jesus rebukes the chief priests and elders of the people for not believing in him and for failing to repent their evil ways.

WEDNESDAY OF THE THIRD WEEK OF ADVENT

If today is December 17 or later, omit these readings and turn to pages 17-21.

READING I Is. 45:6-8, 18, 21-25   **RESP.** Ps. 85:9-10, 11-12, 13-14
GOSPEL Luke 7:18-23

In today's first Scripture reading you will hear the words, "Let justice descend, O heavens, like dew from above . . . let the earth open and salvation bud forth." The liturgy uses these verses frequently during the Advent season. They express the ancient longing of the Jewish people for their Messiah as well, as our own longing for the final coming of Christ. In the responsorial psalm refrain, we once again plead for the coming of Jesus by praying, "Let the clouds rain down the Just One, and the earth bring forth a savior." In the Gospel, Jesus answers the questions from John the Baptist's disciples about whether our Lord is the Messiah they have so long awaited. Instead of giving a direct answer, Jesus describes the things the Old Testament prophets had foretold the Messiah would do. Our Lord then declares that these are the very same things he is doing for the people.

THURSDAY OF THE THIRD WEEK OF ADVENT

If today is December 17 or later, omit these readings and turn to pages 17-21.

READING I Is. 54:1-10   **RESP.** Ps. 30:2 and 4, 5-6, 11-12 and 13
GOSPEL Luke 7:24-30

The first reading for today's Mass takes us back to the closing years of the sixth century before Christ. At this time, the Jews were returning to their homeland in Palestine after a long forced exile in Babylonia. Their land's smaller size and enormous problems had discouraged the Jews. God's prophet consoles them with hope for the future. He assures them that their numbers will increase and that God, who may appear to have abandoned them, will take pity on them and bless them. The Gospel shows us how God's promise ripened in the preaching of John the Baptist that prepared for the saving ministry of Jesus. The responsorial psalm praises God for rescuing his chosen people and changing "my mourning into dancing."

FRIDAY OF THE THIRD WEEK OF ADVENT

If today is December 17 or later, omit these readings and turn to pages 17-21.

| READING I | Is. 56:1-3, 6-8 | RESP. Ps. 67:2-3, 5, 7-8 |
| GOSPEL | John 5:33-36 | |

The first Scripture reading for today's Mass emphasizes the Advent theme that God calls all men to salvation. At the time of Israel's return from the Babylonian exile, the Jews allowed foreigners living within Palestine certain rights and privileges in their community. Today's passage shows that God would extend these benefits even to those outside the promised land — that is, to all who believe in the Lord and keep his commandments. The responsorial psalm refrain also accents this theme of universal salvation as we pray, "O God, let all the nations praise you." In the Gospel, you will hear Jesus referring to the way John the Baptist spoke publicly in our Lord's behalf. Jesus then points out that his miracles are even greater evidence than John's word that he is truly the long-awaited Messiah.

Fourth Week of Advent

FOURTH SUNDAY OF ADVENT — Cycle A

READING I   Is. 7:10-14   RESP. Ps. 24:1-2, 3-4, 5-6
READING II   Rom. 1:1-7
GOSPEL   Matthew 1:18-24

The readings for today's Mass focus on the Blessed Virgin Mary and the mystery of the Nativity, as its liturgical celebration draws steadily nearer. Matthew's Gospel sees in the birth of Jesus the fulfillment of an Old Testament prophecy about a virgin giving birth to a son, whose name Emmanuel means "God is with us." We find the original historical setting of Matthew's quotation in the first reading, which takes us back to the reign of the Jewish King Ahaz some 800 years before Christ. Today's Scripture scholars are not in complete agreement about the virgin-born child's identity or what his birth meant. But since Matthew applies Isaiah's text to the birth of Christ, who is of the House of David, "the sign" God gives Ahaz may concern a child who will continue the bloodline of David. Paul also reminds us that God's Son "was descended from David according to the flesh." The responsorial psalm views the Nativity as an entering into our world of the God who created it, the "king of glory." Through this psalm, the liturgy also exhorts us to prepare our hearts for the Lord's coming by leading sinless lives.

FOURTH SUNDAY OF ADVENT — Cycle B

READING I   2 Sam. 7:1-5, 8-11, 16   RESP. Ps. 89:2-3, 4-5, 27, 29
READING II   Rom. 16:25-27
GOSPEL   Luke 1:26-38

The readings from Scripture for today's Mass pertain to the Blessed Virgin Mary's role in the mystery of the Nativity, as the Christmas liturgy draws near. In his Gospel, Luke tells the familiar story of the angel Gabriel's visit to Mary. She was the one God chose to bring his Son into the world for the first time. The liturgy centers our interest primarily on the fact that Joseph, foster father of Jesus, was of "the House of David" and Mary's child will inherit "the throne of David." In this way, the birth of Jesus fulfilled God's promise, which we find at the end of the Old Testament lesson. Instead of accepting King David's offer to build a house or temple for God, the Lord promises to maintain David's own house or family down through the ages. The responsorial psalm also takes up this theme in the verse, "I have sworn to David my servant: Forever will I confirm your posterity." Paul then shows that God unveiled his secret plan of salvation for the gentiles only after the birth of Christ. The apostle preached this "mystery hidden for many ages," and we are among those who will gain eternal life if we are faithful to his message.

FOURTH SUNDAY OF ADVENT — Cycle C

READING I Micah 5:1-4	RESP. Ps. 80:2-3, 15-16, 18-19
READING II Heb. 10:5-10	
GOSPEL Luke 1:39-45	

Today's readings focus on the Blessed Virgin Mary and the announcement of our Lord's birth. Luke's Gospel strikes the keynote by describing Mary's visit to Elizabeth. When we hear Elizabeth speak of "the mother of my Lord" and "the fruit of your womb," our thoughts turn naturally to the mystery of Christmas. In Mary's faith and obedience, we see the conditions God required for coming to dwell among us. This theme of obedience also appears in the reading from Paul. He gives us the whole reason for the Nativity, namely, that Christ came to sanctify us "through the offering of [his] body." Paul builds upon a text from Psalm 40: "I [Christ] have come to do your will." In the Old Testament lesson, our Christian faith finds a prophecy of the birth, in Bethlehem, of Jesus, "who is to be ruler in Israel" and who shall "shepherd his flock by the strength of the Lord." The responsorial psalm takes up these themes by calling on God as the "shepherd of Israel," who protects "the son of man whom you yourself made strong." We also hear the Advent cry, "Rouse your power, and come to save us."

DECEMBER 17 — WEEKDAY OF ADVENT

READING I Gen. 49:2, 8-10	RESP. Ps. 72:3-4, 7-8, 17
GOSPEL Matthew 1:1-17	

In today's Mass the Scripture readings remind us that Jesus was a member of King David's royal family as God promised the Messiah would be. In the first passage, we meet Jacob, an ancestor of Jesus, who tells his sons, "The scepter shall never depart from Judah." A scepter was a staff that a ruler carried as a symbol of authority. In this way, Jacob indicates the supremacy of the tribe of Judah over all other tribes of Israel. Since King David was a member of the tribe of Judah, the passage shows God choosing David's family for the Messiah. In the Gospel, we hear St. Matthew's account of the ancestry of Christ. Matthew establishes the two requirements for the Messiah. First, he must be a true Israelite who can trace his lineage to Abraham. Second, his family line must descend from King David. The responsorial psalm describes the blessings in the age of the Messiah.

DECEMBER 18 — WEEKDAY OF ADVENT

READING I Jer. 23:5-8
GOSPEL Matthew 1:18-24
RESP. Ps. 72:1, 12-13, 18-19

Today's readings teach us how our Lord fulfilled the prophecies that the Messiah would come from King David's family. The first passage tells about this in the imagery of a family tree that is common even today. God promises through his prophet Jeremiah that he will raise up "a righteous shoot" (or branch) from the family tree of David. This future king, the Messiah, "shall reign and govern wisely." The responsorial psalm accents this theme by saying of God's king, "He shall govern your people with justice." The Gospel also shows how Jeremiah's prophecy about David's royal line came true. In Matthew's account of our Lord's birth, an angel refers to Joseph as "the son of David." Thus the Son of God has become man legally in the family of David through Joseph his foster-father, and naturally through Mary — as Luke's Gospel indicates.

DECEMBER 19 — WEEKDAY OF ADVENT

READING I Judg. 13:2-7, 24-25
GOSPEL Luke 1:5-25
RESP. Ps. 71:3-4, 5-6, 16-17

The Scripture readings today tell matching stories about the births of two important people involved in saving mankind from its sinfulness. The first reading tells the story of the birth of Samson, and the Gospel describes the birth of John the Baptist. You will notice a number of strikingly similar events in each of these stories. An angel comes to announce the news of each child's birth as someone whom God has set apart for a special mission to the Jewish people. Since each mother had previously been unable to have children, her pregnancy is evidence of

God's special favor and purpose at work in her life. God invites each child to live a life of total dedication to his special calling. We may regard the responsorial psalm as a prayer from Samson and John, asking the Lord to help them carry out the assignments he has destined them for.

DECEMBER 20 — WEEKDAY OF ADVENT

READING I   Is. 7:10-14   **RESP.** Ps. 24:1-2, 3-4, 5-6
GOSPEL   Luke 1:26-38

Today's readings focus on an underlying theme of this season — how the Messiah was born of a virgin. In the first passage, God assures the Jewish King Ahaz that the throne of Judah will not go vacant because God has promised to continue the royal family of David forever. God gives the sign of a child whose name Immanuel means "God is with us." St. Matthew in his Gospel relates this prophecy to the birth of Jesus from the Virgin Mary. The responsorial psalm is one that the Jews sang during processions into the temple. In the words, "Let the Lord enter," the liturgy discovers a plea for the coming of Christ into our hearts through the graces of Christmas. The Gospel tells how God invited Mary to become the Mother of the Messiah. Some scholars find in the angel's greeting, "The Lord is with you," a reference to the Immanuel who God said would one day come to his people.

DECEMBER 21 — WEEKDAY OF ADVENT

See next page for alternate readings for December 21.

READING I   Song. 2:8-14   **RESP.** Ps. 33:2-3, 11-12, 20-21
GOSPEL   Luke 1:39-45

The theme of joy runs through the Scripture readings for today's Mass. By continually sounding this note of joy, the liturgy encourages us to anticipate eagerly the joys of the Christmas season just a few days away. These joys are primarily spiritual, as we recall the way God showed his great love for us by becoming man. To develop this theme, the liturgy selects for the first reading one of the many love songs in the lyrical Song of Songs in the Old Testament. The girl talking in this passage symbolizes the Jewish people, and her lover represents God. The season of springtime is a further symbol that God expects to renew Israel when he comes as Messiah. The responsorial psalm accents this theme of joy in saying, "Cry out with joy in the Lord." In the Gospel, we share the joy

Elizabeth experienced when Mary visited her.

READING I Zeph. 3:14-18 **RESP. Ps. 33:2-3, 11-12, 20-21**
GOSPEL Luke 1:39-45

The theme of joy runs through the Scripture readings for today's Mass. By continually sounding this note of joy, the liturgy encourages us to anticipate eagerly the joys of the Christmas season just a few days away. These joys are primarily spiritual, as we recall the way God showed his great love for us by becoming man. To develop this theme, the liturgy invites us to listen to a joyful message from the prophet Zephaniah in the first reading. He calls the Jewish people to proclaim their joy because the Lord has forgiven them. Especially appropriate for this season is what the prophet says about the Lord God being in the midst of his people as a mighty savior who renews them by his love. The responsorial psalm accents this theme of joy by inviting us to "cry out with joy in the Lord." In the Gospel, we share Elizabeth's joy when Mary visited her.

DECEMBER 22 — WEEKDAY OF ADVENT

READING I 1 Sam. 1:24-28 **RESP. Ps. 1 Sam. 2:1, 4-5, 6-7, 8**
GOSPEL Luke 1:46-56

The responsorial psalm and the Gospel for today's Mass present two inspiring prayers of praise to God by women who were important figures in the history of man's salvation. The first prayer is that of Hannah, the mother of Samuel. He was the man who anointed David as king of Israel. We will respond to the first reading by saying Hannah's prayer. The reading itself tells us what prompted Hannah to pray this way. She had brought her baby Samuel to the temple and dedicated him to the service of God. She did this to thank God for allowing her to have a child. The Gospel passage contains the prayer of praise Mary spoke when she arrived at the house of her cousin Elizabeth. The liturgy uses this hymn, which we call the Magnificat, in her evening prayer of Vespers.

DECEMBER 23 — WEEKDAY OF ADVENT

READING I Mal. 3:1-4, 23-24   **RESP.** Ps. 25:4-5, 8-9, 10, 14
GOSPEL Luke 1:57-66

The first Scripture reading for today's Mass calls our attention to a special messenger who will prepare the Jewish people for the coming of the Messiah. We hear the prophet Malachi identify this person as the prophet Elijah. This passage apparently had a strong influence in creating the people's expectation at the time of Jesus that Elijah would return one day to announce the coming of the Messiah. The Gospel tells us about the birth of John the Baptist. We know he was the messenger that Malachi spoke about because Jesus told his disciples that John had fulfilled the destiny of Elijah. John's mission was to proclaim repentance — a reminder for us today to prepare our own hearts for the graces of the Christmas season. The responsorial psalm also anticipates the approaching feast of Christ's birth in the refrain, "Your redemption is near at hand."

DECEMBER 24 — WEEKDAY OF ADVENT

READING I 2 Sam. 7:1-5, 8-12, 14, 16   **RESP.** Ps. 89:2-3, 4-5, 27, 29
GOSPEL Luke 1:67-79

The Scripture readings for today's final Mass of the Advent season focus our attention on God's promise to send a Messiah for his people from the family line of King David. The first passage takes us back to the time when David had overcome many of his enemies. The king began to think of building a temple where his people could worship God. The Lord indicated to David through the king's friend, the prophet Nathan, his own wishes about this project. God then promised to continue the house of David forever. Our response to this reading highlights this theme with the words, "Forever will I confirm your posterity." The Gospel contains the hymn of praise that Zechariah, the father of John the Baptist, prayed when the boy received the name John at his circumcision. In the opening lines, you will hear Zechariah refer to God's promise to bring salvation to his people through David.